novum 🐟 pocket

Philomena Schley

The Travails of a Black African Woman

novum ▲ pocket

© 2023 novum publishing

ISBN 978-3-903468-01-6
Cover photo:
Vadim Tissen | Dreamstime.com
Cover design, layout & typesetting:
novum publishing
Author's photo: Philomena Schley

www.novum-publishing.co.uk

Climate neutral
Print product
ClimatePartner.com/16547-2201-1002

Contents

Biography

As a child born in Africa, raised by a single mother who truly cares for her children, a mother who knows when her children are hungry and think of what to do, a mother who doesn't care whether it's raining or sunny, she goes out to look for something for her children to eat. I do not have enough words to describe her. That was my mother, a black African woman.

The True Story of Me

A six years old girl child born in Benin City, Edo State, Nigeria, I had a mother and a younger sister called Martha; both of us were with my mother. My mother trades in food, buying from farmers and selling to consumers. She normally goes around with a female taxi driver, which was uncommon at that time. Her business was so stressful that she always returned late at night. I helped her with the cooking and other domestic work at home, such as fetching water, buying firewood and washing clothes. Her daily task of providing for her household took hold of her emotions, sometimes making her unhappy. Looking at her face, I can tell when she is not happy. As young as I was at that time, my mother would give me money to go to the market and buy food and, after buying it, I would cook the food if she was not at home to assist me. We go to the neighbourhood to fetch water with buckets; we have a very big drum at home to fill.

Living in Lagos, Nigeria, with my Aunt

As the burden became too heavy to bear, my mother decided to seek help from her relatives. One day, she was thinking of looking for someone to take care of us, so she went to the village to discuss it with her brother's wife. My mother had a half-sister in Lagos who was looking for someone to help her with household chores. She came to Benin to meet my mother, and my mother gave me to her to help her with household chores and also for her to put me in school in Lagos. We got to my step-aunt's house in Lagos; it was two rooms, one sitting room and one bedroom. But I usually slept with a mat on the carpet in the sitting room.

Every morning, I woke up early, prepared food in the kitchen, and did the house chores. When I finished, my aunty gave me my food, which I ate in the kitchen. Later, my cousin came and joined me. We were doing it together, and it was ok, but my aunt did not enrol me in any school. My aunt's husband liked to celebrate or go out and enjoy himself with his friends or relatives at home, so I usually ran a lot of errands for them. At times when I bought many items, the seller would give me one drink, which I would drink there immediately, because if my aunt saw me, she would beat me. My step-aunt would prepare fufu [cassava flour] or semovita with assorted meat and soup for the visitors. The music would be very loud. Later we would pack the plates and wash and clean everywhere. All this was fun and good.

Later, I started thinking about my not going to school, and my mother hadn't come to Lagos to see me either, though my senior brother came one day. He did not see anything wrong with my not going to school; he did not even ask me because they were all blinded by Lagos life, where people were happy to live and see their family take care of you. After staying for some days, he left, and I was still there.

Back to my mother's place in Benin City

After three years of living with my step-aunt without going to school, my mother came to Lagos with a baby boy on her back. She asked me if everything was ok, and I said yes. I told her if she was leaving, I would go with her. She said no, and I said ok. The next day, I woke up along with her as she arranged her things and prepared herself to leave for Benin City. Immediately after she left the house, I followed her. I was walking behind her as she went to the bus station though she did not see me. She entered the bus, and I also entered from the back of the bus; then she saw me and was shocked, but she could not tell the bus driver to stop because he was already moving. That was how I came back to Benin. When we got to Benin, my mother said I had to go back to Lagos because she was afraid of what her relatives and family in the village would say. I told her I was not going back. So she asked me to hide in the house of her lady friend who has no child of her own in the meantime, in case her family asked after my whereabouts, she would tell them I ran away. After a week, I came back to live in my mother's house.

Visiting my Uncle gradually

I lived with my mother for about a year, then in 1974, her younger brother came back from Canada, and we started going to his house to visit him. At times, we would sleep over, and at times we would go back that same day. He was living alone with his two sons, and I did not really understand why because I was still a child. After frequent visits for some time, I started living with my uncle, along with his children and my senior uncle. My uncle was a very proud man, though very educated. So many of the family members were happy to have a brother like him who was educated and studied overseas. I was doing all the domestic chores in my uncle's house, and when school resumed a new session, he enrolled me in a primary school, and I was very happy even though I had to walk to the school.

Later, I had to go back to live with my mother because my cousins' mother came to start living with them. I started primary school not very far from my house, and later we moved to another house near the market. There were a lot of people in that area, and the road was a busy place, with people going and coming. One of our relative's houses was not far from us, so we used to walk to her house and visit her. She was a very nice woman and godly; she loved her family and made people happy. Whenever she saw us, she was always happy and tried to do one thing or the other for us. When we were through visiting her, I would go home or play with friends.

Visiting grandma

When I was on holiday, my mother would take me to the village to visit and stay with my grandmother for a while. I was always very happy when I got to the village. My grandmother also was always very happy. If it was a market day, she would cook rice, but on normal days she would make normal food, but mostly rice because she knew I like rice. On days that were not market days, we went to the farm. On the farm, she would work, and I would also help her to work because the farm was given to her by her stepson. She planted tomatoes and other crops. After working on the farm, she would put firewood on my head, and we would walk home. On our way home, as the sun was going down, birds would be singing, and my grandma understood the language of the birds. A voice from one of the birds would make my grandmother say she was going to have a visitor, so she needed to run home. True to her prediction, when we got home, we would see a visitor waiting for her.

She would be very happy, and she would say to me, "Didn't I tell you I would have a visitor today?"

In the evening, she would cook for the two of us to eat, and later in the night she would light a fire in the room because of the cold weather. We would sit by the fireplace, and she started telling me stories, advising me on the issues of life, and telling me that life was not easy. After the stories, we would go to bed.

While still in the village, my grandmother would send me to the river to fetch water. One of the rivers was very far, and she would pack the dirty clothes for me to go and wash in the river. I usually went along with my village friends, and when I was going, my grandmother would give me some garri (cassava flakes) with coconut or dried fish so I wouldn't be hungry. We normally ate the garri with our hands because spoons were not so common; it was an item for the rich in Africa at that time.

The road to the streams in Africa was narrow and full of trees and animals; birds were busy singing everywhere, and even snakes crossed the road. Most times, we would have to rest along the way before continuing the journey to the river, and by the time we got close, we would have to climb down a very steep hill. When we finally reached the river, we put down the loads of clothes on our heads and started washing with our local soap. The river water was very beautiful, you could see the fish swimming; we drank from the water and my friends swam in it. While they were swimming, I would stand by the bank of the river and look at them because I could not swim; I was afraid of the water.

When I was through, I would have to wait for others so we could all go back home together. We had to climb the hill to get back home; it was very difficult climbing the hill with a heavy load of clothes on our heads. The distance from the river to the village was about 5km, and we normally walked that distance in our bare feet; there was no footwear. When I got home, my grandmother would help me to get the load of clothes down from my head.

She would greet me, saying I have done well. I rested a little before going to spread the clothes on the rope for the sun's rays to dry them up. The next day, I checked if the clothes were dried; if they were, I would remove them from the rope, fold them and give them back to grandmother to keep in her local box. Then, after about a week or two, my grandmother would ask me if I could go to the river again to wash the dirty clothes.

In the morning, after doing the house chores on the days I wasn't going to the river, I would walk around visiting my girlfriends; we would go out and play in the street. If it was night, the moon would be shining because there was no electricity in the entire village. We would play, sing and be happy. At times my friends' mothers would join us in our games, and when we were tired, we would go to our various homes and sleep. My friends saw me as a city girl, a very important person with a city lifestyle; their grandmothers used to call me and give me gifts.

After the holidays, my mother would ask the lady driver that used to drive her from the city to the village to take me back to the city if she was not able to come for me herself. When I got to the city with the driver, I would stop at the market square and play with my friends and family members before going home because the market was not far from our house. My mother was a very popular woman, and everyone in the market would keep asking after her. When I finally got to the house, I would do other things that my younger sister could not do by herself.

Living with my Uncle fully

After some years, my mum had to move to another house, still one room, because that was all the rent she could afford. Then she asked me to go and stay with my uncle fully. I was staying with him; he lived 20km away from my mother's house. He had lots of girlfriends because he liked women. Anytime he brought a girl home, I would make sure I prepared food and kept it in the flask because he liked it hot. I just had to do it because, for me, I didn't see it as something too important; it was just normal for me.

My uncle's house was like living in Europe, a very big difference from my mother's house; although it was also rented, the house was more beautiful than my mother's house. I was very happy staying with my uncle because staying with someone who came from abroad or studied abroad attracted a lot of respect from people around me.

My uncle enrolled me in a government school that was not very far from the house. My uncle's children were attending a private school, and they went to school in a car while I used my legs to walk to school because they were not my parents. But they were very nice to me; they did not discriminate against me in other areas. The children played with me, and they did not treat me like a stranger.

After a while, my uncle relocated to another city called Sapele as a secondary school teacher and came to Benin every two weeks, so I started staying with my senior uncle. When I finished primary 5, I had to leave Benin and live with my uncle in Sapele because he was made the vice-principal of the school. I started my first year in the same secondary school my uncle was in. I was a day student because I had to go home and do the house chores after school. In my second year, I had to move into the boarding school, in this same school, because my uncle was transferred to another city called Asaba. In the boarding house, my uncle helped me with food, and my mother helped with some items. Later on, I left the boarding school in Sapele and went to live with my uncle in Asaba. He was living outside the school premises. After a while again, he relocated back to Benin City with a new wife, two additional children and the two boys he had before, though the two boys had grown. The second wife was very nice and helpful, and we understood each other. The house we were staying in belonged to one of our relatives.

Later my uncle built his own house in Benin, and we all moved to the new house. My uncle's children were now attending a government school, and I was also attending a different government school, which was very far from our house. I had to walk in the morning for about 5km from the house, then take a bus for about 10km, take another bus for about 8km or more, then walk another 5km to get to school. By the time I got to school, all the other children would already be learning in class. If the teacher was in class, I would not enter. Instead, I would go and hide, and then when the teacher left, I would enter the class, though the teacher used to come back later to find out if I had come to class and, when he saw me, he would still flog me with a cane. After all the teaching and beating, I would still have to sit down and learn because if I didn't, I would be doing it myself. I don't have a father, and my mother cannot be responsible for my upkeep, though, at that time, school fees were free. If not, I don't think I would have been able to go to school; I really thank God for it. So I had to go to school so I could have a certificate to be able to get a job after school.

When I was in class four, my uncle's second wife left him, and my grandmother was already living with my uncle in Benin City, so I had to stand in as a mother for them because the second wife's children were still very young.

My Uncle's third Wife

I took over the duty of running the house until my uncle married a third wife. Even with the third wife at home, my uncle was still giving me money for the house feeding until I had an ugly experience with his new wife; my uncle gave me money to go to the market and buy food. When I came back from the market, I kept the food in the kitchen. When it was time for me to cook, the food was missing; I looked for it everywhere, but I could not find it. I asked everybody, but nobody admitted that they had taken it; I started crying because such a thing had never happened in the house before. I went to check my uncle's cupboard in his room, and I saw the food there. When my uncle came back, I told him everything that had happened. He did not ask me anything, nor did he ask his new wife; instead, he called me to where he was and beat me up seriously, put a chair in my hand and asked me to kneel down and raise my hand up with the chair in my hands. I was very angry, and I told him I didn't want to live with him any more. I packed my belongings and he threw them outside in the rain. I packed my wet belongings and left my uncle's house. I did not know what to do; life was really hard for me.

I Met Kelly's father

A week after I left my uncle's house, I met a man named Kito; he said he had just come back from overseas. He smoked and dressed like someone who came from overseas. He told me he had been in Germany; we fell in love, and I stayed with him because I did not have any other place to go to. I couldn't go to my mother's place because she was angry with me for leaving my uncle's place. So I had to live with him as my boyfriend, even though he was living with his friends. At times, his friends would tell him to leave; he would leave that friend's place and go to another friend's place because he said he was working on travelling papers for people who wanted to travel out of the country. He was young and good-looking.

Later on, he said to me, "I will help you to get a passport, and you will travel with me overseas."

I was very happy. I never knew he was in an Asylum in Deutschland, not until one of his friends mentioned it. He usually goes to see his mother, or the mother will come and see him at his friend's place, though she was always saying that I was not good enough for her son. Whenever his mother came around, she would bring food and give him some money for his pocket because he did not have money; he only got money whenever he did travelling documents for people, though most times he could not finish them. He got my passport, and when my passport was ready, he said I should look for money to assist him. I sold my clothes as second-hand, borrowed money from my mother's cousin, added it to the money from my clothes and gave it to him. He added his own and bought the tickets. Though I didn't know where he got his own money from; probably from the travelling documents he did for people.

Landed in Liberia

We travelled out, but unfortunately for us, we landed in Liberia, and we were stranded there. The first day we stayed in a hotel, the next day there was no money again. He had to look for someone to stay with. Liberia was a beautiful place, and the people were very good. They helped us because he was always telling them that he would travel out of the country, but later on he bought bags and shoes for Nigeria. He sold everything, but what he did with the money, I don't know. I couldn't cope with the situation because he didn't have his own rented apartment, so we kept moving from one part of the city to another. Later, he bought tickets for us, and we travelled out of Liberia, though I didn't know where to until we got to the airport and took a flight out of Liberia to another country called DDR.

My first time in Germany

When we got there, I didn't know he came to seek Asylum. They allowed me into one of the cities, though today I can't remember the name of the city because then everything was looking very strange to me. They didn't allow us to live together. That was the day I knew what Asylum was. We were lined up with people from different countries, and I was living in another city. The room I was living in was filled with German women who slept with different men.

One day, Kito called me and said that we should move back to Nigeria, saying that the sister who lives in America said we should come to America and that America is better than Germany. I was very happy, thinking he was telling me the truth. I never knew he was deceiving me because in Germany, you couldn't speak English, and I couldn't speak German at that time. So I went to the office and told them I wanted to leave for Nigeria, and they said ok. They bought a ticket for me, and I left for Nigeria.

Back to Nigeria

I was the one who got to Nigeria first and stayed two weeks before he came. His nephew, who was working at the airport, helped us and gave him one room from his two-room apartment to stay in because he thought we wouldn't stay too long, but we had to stay there for a long time.

One day, he told his nephew that he wanted to go to Benin and buy tickets for us to travel to America. So he left for Benin. I waited for him to come back as promised, but he didn't. I was now ashamed of myself, so I travelled to Benin to look for him. When I got to Benin, a family friend took me to where he was staying. When I got there, I found him drinking, smoking and enjoying himself. I was very angry. I stayed for a while, and then we travelled back to Lagos to pack our things from his nephew's place, but we had no place to go, so one of his friends gave him some money to rent a house; he rented one room in Lagos. After the money was gone, there was no money to renew the rent, and I had to go and live with one of the brothers in Lagos, though I do not know how they were related. We moved to their house and started living with them, and then I got pregnant with Kelly. I didn't have any money, and I was wearing one blouse and tying one wrapper. I had to think of what to eat; the woman I was staying with was very good to me even though they did not have enough money to live well. When I saw that living was difficult, I had to resort to begging because the lady had done her best for me. I thanked her from the bottom of my heart. I had to leave her house and relocate to another house. Kito went out every night to work, but the money he received was not enough; it could only pay for a one-room apartment. The money was not enough to feed us, but because I was pregnant, there was a Yoruba man in the neighbourhood who was giving me five nairas (N5) to eat every day, because the Yorubas are very sympathetic to their fellow humans.

One day, as I was sleeping, I heard a knock on the door, and I asked, "Who is that?"

The person said, "It's me, your mother."

The one room we rented had no bed, just carpet and a mat on the floor. So when I saw my mother with one of my old girlfriends, tears flowed out of my eyes. I cried out loudly; she held me close and said I must follow her back to Benin City. I said ok because the suffering was becoming unbearable. I was really thankful to God that my mother came.

Back to my mother's house in Benin City

I followed my mother to her house in Benin. We took almost five buses to get there. When we got to Benin, I was very ashamed of myself, but what could I do? My mother later told me that she sent the Police to arrest Kito's mother, and when I asked why, she said it was because they had been looking for me everywhere. I told her she shouldn't have done that because the woman did not know where I was. I was angry, so I asked her to tell the police to release her.

Living with Kito's parents

Later, I decided to go to my boyfriend's mother's house. She had two small children living with her and her husband; they didn't have their own house, they rented two rooms. When I got there, I knelt down and begged them, and I moved in with them. I had to sleep at the back of the bed because I was pregnant, while the two small children slept on the floor.

Kito's mother kept asking me why I got pregnant by her son. She felt the son was a good man, living overseas, so he deserved a better person. I was living with them and enduring all the insults from them, but life was so hard for them, too, so after some time, I left the house with my son; by then I had given birth to Kelly.

Kito was still in Lagos all this while I was with the parents. Later, he relocated to Benin, and my son and I went to live with him. We rented a one-room apartment with no bed, just carpet and a mat to sleep on. I tried going to the market to sell items, and I started getting a little money to pay for the house rent. Kito would leave in the morning to go and visit his friends and would not return until evening. We fought most of the time, and I hated myself because I couldn't even buy a roll-on for my armpit, nor toothpaste to brush our teeth, nor could I afford a special cream to rub on my body. If I was on my menses, I would use toilet roll, and I used to pray to God and ask when all this suffering would end.

One day, we fought again; I insulted him, and then he beat me up, so I took my son Kelly, left the house we rented, went to my mother's house and started living there. My relatives started laughing and mocking me, saying I did not look like someone who travelled overseas. I had no job and nothing to do, but God Almighty helped me through the lawyer's mother, who was living in the house opposite my mother's house. She asked me if I could help her to clean her house and, at times, go to the market for her. I said no problem, I agreed and started. She was buying baby food for my son, who was still very small at that time, and he was very handsome. When I was working for her, I would go and take care of my son or take him along at times. Sometimes we travelled with her daughter, who was a court magistrate in Ekpoma, Edo State. Her daughter would take good care of us, and when we were returning to Benin from Ekpoma, she would buy me food and give me money. Life was better.

I did the job until my son was about two years old. He was attending a kindergarten school near the house, and the school owner came and took him to school and also brought him back. After some years, the lawyer's mother relocated to Asaba, her hometown. Life was not easy again, though my son and I used to go and visit her in Asaba. When we returned, she would give me some money to take care of myself and my son. After a while, I stopped visiting her for reasons I can't even tell. I looked for another job in a restaurant in Benin City. I was cooking in the restaurant, but life was very hard, so I stopped working there. I also packed my things and left my mother's house to live with a family friend in another part of the city, the place I had stayed before when I left my uncle's house. After a while, I left my son with the woman and went to another town in Benin called Okomu to look for a job because I needed to earn money; life was very difficult.

I was in a nearby village called Oko. There, at 5am, I had to wake up with my girlfriend; we were sharing the same room. I knew her in Okada, the village I lived in before, in the name of looking for money. I was frying akara (bean balls) in the village, and later on they said I should come and see the night men; I couldn't, so I decided to pack up the frying pan. This lady then asked me to come to okomu, and we started living together in one room, sharing the rent money. At times she went to her village to bring food. We slept in the same bed. In the morning, we would wake up by 5am to prepare and meet the truck at 6am. The truck was always filled with both men and women; we had to stand inside the truck till we got to Okomu.

When the truck arrived at Okomu, everybody would get down from the truck and move to their various departments to work. My girlfriend and I worked in the same department; the company was a palm oil farm; we had to go into the bush, between the palm trees and then rub chemicals on them to prevent weeds from growing on them. It was a difficult job, and I was always afraid of the bush because of the wild animals, like snakes, bush rats, etc. When I finished my day's work, I would go and ask my girlfriend if she was also through, and when she was, we would both walk to where the truck was, enter, and the truck would take us back home. When we got to the house, we would take off our clothes, take a bath, look for something to eat and then rest for the night.

The next day, we resumed the same routine till the end of the month, when we got our pay slips to see how much money we had earned, and I was always happy when I got my money at the end of the month. I would send some of the money to the old woman taking care of my son in Benin City and also buy food for her when I was going to Benin. At times I would go and spend two or three days with my son before returning to Udo for the Okomu job. This was what I was doing for a while, and I was happy until one day my mother came to see me at my workplace in Okomu and told me that my senior brother, who came from Austria, wanted to see me. I followed my mother, hoping he would help me to travel out of Nigeria. One of my mother's neighbours went with me to see him; when we got to where my senior brother was staying with my uncle from Canada, who I used to stay with, I knelt down and begged him to help me.

He said to me, "Someone who has given birth cannot go overseas." I cried seriously when I heard those words. My mother's neighbour who went with me told me not to cry, that as long as there is life, things will get better and that I should take things easy. My mother tried to ask him why he had forgotten that I used to squeeze money out from the money my uncle would give me to buy food and send it to him whenever I saw anyone who came from Austria to Nigeria for a visit.

Whenever my older brother paid a visit to Nigeria from Austria, he would bring some clothes for his friends, but me as his stepsister, he would not give me anything, only once he mistakenly gave me a pair of yellow lady's shoes, but he came back to collect them, I had to return to my work at Udo.

After a while, my uncle helped me to get a job at Bendel Line Transport Company in Benin because his friend was the director of the company. I worked there for two years, and we drove buses from one part of the state to another; the job was not difficult, but it did not last long; the company was having problems, and most times I would come back very late. At that time, my son was now living with my mum.

Back to Lagos

I left the Bendel line job and travelled to Lagos to start living with a family friend who owns a restaurant in Badagry. I decided to assist her in running the restaurant. After some months, someone told her that there was a vacancy for a receptionist in a hotel if I would like to take the job. I agreed, and I was very happy. The hotel was not that beautiful or clean, but I didn't have a choice. I was working with other people there, and we understood each other.

After some months, I travelled to Benin for a visit. My mother was outside, sitting down on a small stool. When she saw me, she was very happy; I bought a mattress for her from Lagos. I spent one week with my family, and then I had to go back to Lagos and resume my work.

One month later, I visited my family again and decided to visit a family friend, Mr. Asien, who helped Kelly's father before in Germany, because the brother told me he was asking after me. He told me he had a German friend named Stefan, and they work for him in Blumengarten. He showed me two of his pictures and said he had told him about me, and that his friend is interested in me and will help me to travel to Germany, though he is much older than me.

I met Stefan

Stefan and I exchanged a series of letters, and in one of the letters, he told me he had a father, a mother and a sister, and that he also had a house. I didn't care much about what he had because I was already in love with him. We communicated for about one year, and in the last letter he wrote to me, he told me he would be coming to Nigeria to marry me; I was very happy. My family friend, Mr. Asien, his wife and Stefan came to Nigeria. We all stayed in a hotel. He bought a nightgown for me, which I wore to go out. He told me it was a nightgown and was meant to be worn inside the house at night. I told him that in Nigeria; we don't care much about what we are putting on and that it's normal for us to wear nightwear at any time of the day. I also bought African clothes and made it down for both of us. I took them to see my mother; my mother had already invited friends and relatives to her house, and some of her neighbour's children were standing outside the house. My mother asked my junior sister to prepare food, and a white man and her sister were coming to visit. After we visited my mother, we went back to the hotel.

The next day, we visited my uncle, who lives in Benin, because he was the one who would stand in as my father at the registry office since I no longer had a father.

The next day, Stefan and I woke up on time, dressed up in the native attire I made before they came to Nigeria.

Mr. Asien and his wife also put on their own native attire. We chartered a taxi to the venue of the registry marriage. Stefan also gave me 3,000 DM, which I gave to Mr. Asien to appreciate him for all the help he rendered to me.

Marrying a white man

We drove to the marriage venue. My mother was already there, dressed in her native attire, and my younger sister and two of my family members represented my father, and Mr. Asien and his wife were there. The representatives of the marriage registry were just two men, and one of them asked us if we wanted to get married; we said yes. Stefan brought the ring he had brought from Germany out of his pocket, and he gave it to the man; the man put the ring on the table and asked me if I wanted to become Stefan's wife. I said yes. When I said yes, I looked at Stefan; he was looking old, but in Africa, it was normal. Though people in Africa will call him my sugar daddy, I didn't mind as long as he could take good care of me. Later, the registry man asked us to get up, and he asked Stefan to take my hand and put the ring on my finger. I also put a ring on his finger, and the man pronounced us man and wife. My younger sister prepared rice and brought it to the guesthouse. We bought some drinks from them; we ate and left the guesthouse. I was very happy that everything went well.

After a week, Stefan left Nigeria with the Asiens back to Germany. After Stefan left, I went back to my mother's house, and my mother asked me if the white man was not too old for me. I told her that he was better than all the black men who could not take care of their wives, and she said I was right.

When Stefan got to Germany, he wrote me, and I also wrote him, thanking him for coming. I was now living in Benin with one of my girlfriends while waiting for my visa to come. After waiting for some time, my visa was ready, and I went to the embassy, collected my visa and travelled to Germany.

Back to Germany

When I got to Germany, Stefan and Mr. Asien were at the airport waiting for me. When they saw me, they embraced me, then took me away from the airport. On the way, they were speaking German, so I didn't understand what they were saying. I was wearing a long gown, blue shoes and a jacket. The shoes were hurting my feet. As we got to Stefan's house, I saw his parents, who were both old. He took my bag upstairs, and I was still sitting with his parents downstairs. Stefan's sister Emilia was also around to see me, and she tried to speak English because Stefan was speaking English to me, though not perfectly. They prepared food, but I couldn't eat at first; later I went upstairs. Stefan showed me the wardrobe. It was an old wardrobe though, he asked me to arrange my clothes there, and I did. At night, we slept together in the same bed. Stefan had a lot of African film cassettes, which we watched together. He tried to explain the films to me; sometimes I would understand, and sometimes I wouldn't, and I would then demonstrate to him with my hands what I was trying to say.

Stefan was on a two-week holiday, and he spent it with me before returning to work. When he went to work, I would come downstairs and help the parents to do some house chores and prepare meals. Their meals were very difficult to prepare, though Stefan had previously bought rice, saying that in Nigeria, we eat rice a lot. Stefan's sister usually baked cakes and brought them to us because she lived in the same village as us. When I was with Stefan's mother in the kitchen, she tried to explain some things to me in German; if I did not understand, I would wait until Stefan came back; she would repeat what she said, and he would explain it to me. The mother was having pains in her legs, so she couldn't walk properly, and the father had a lung problem as well.

Later on, Stefan sent me to a retired German school teacher to register with her. When we got to the teacher's house, she spoke English to me because since I came to Germany, I could not really speak the way I wanted to. She asked me how I knew Stefan, and what was my reason for marrying him, because she could see that he was a little too old for me. I said yes, but in Africa it's not a problem, and I told her a parable that my mother told me in Nigeria. She gave me the date and time to resume, which she wrote on a small piece of paper so I would see it clearly. Later Stefan and I left the woman's place, and he told me to try and learn Dutch very well so as to communicate with his parents when he is not around, and also for future purposes. Sometimes, if I follow Stefan to buy things from the stores, people who know him would look at me because it's a small village.

Stefan's house has a dove house inside the garden. Every evening, we go to the dove house, and I give them food and water. He gave names to all the doves; one of them was called Mercy, and any time he called the name, the dove would fly and perch on his head; it was really funny. At times, I would follow him to the garden to help him in cleaning it; especially at weekends when he had more time. I also planted crops in the garden, which I always watered.

I started attending my German class lessons; Stefan would drop me there, but after some time, he stopped, and I would walk there because it was not very far. Two months after arriving in Germany, I got pregnant. Stefan was shocked; he said he did not believe the child was his. He brought out a microscope to see; he took his sperm and put it on the microscope to see if his sperm would swim – I just looked at him. Then he said his cousin's sister didn't have a child and that when I gave birth to the child, she would come and adopt it. I told him his cousin would not be adopting my child; I was very angry. I started asking myself what was even wrong with these men. I don't understand them, because since I came to Germany, he did not see me with another man. I still continued with my German class lessons at Mrs. Ella's house.

Stefan's father was a good man. When he saw that I was pregnant, he started giving me 200DM every month. At times he would ask me to go out and take a walk, but I didn't because I didn't have any friends, though I was hoping that maybe one day I would have. Stefan's father registered me in a bank so I could save my money there; I knew I was in for better things to come. I would send some of that money to Nigeria for Kelly's school fees and feeding money for my family.

That year, while I was pregnant, I told him I had a son in Nigeria. He said if I liked, I could bring my family to Germany, because my family friend who introduced me to him told him that my family was not that rich. I told him we were not rich, and that we were just able to feed ourselves. My mother was the only one taking care of the rest of my family members in Nigeria, and I was missing them very much. At times I would be crying because there was nobody to talk to; I was alone, and nobody understood. The worst was that Stefan's apartment was upstairs, with a parlour, bedroom, and kitchen, which was very small, and a bathroom with a glass door separating it from the kitchen. You could see the person in the bathroom when you were in the kitchen. I was not cooking upstairs; I helped the mother to cook, and we ate downstairs. I told Stefan we should be eating upstairs at times, but he disagreed with me; even when I cooked in the kitchen upstairs, we would still bring it downstairs to eat, but any time the mother's friend from childhood was around, he would ask me to stay upstairs because if she saw me, she would go and broadcast it round the whole village that she saw Stefan's wife. I was not going out much because I didn't know many people. Communicating with my family in Nigeria was also very difficult, as phones were very expensive. At times I would write letters, but the letters would take a very long time to get to Nigeria.

Stefan usually took me to visit his cousins and aunt. Any time I visited them, they would buy me clothes and try to make me happy. Stefan did not have any friends except Hans, his childhood friend; he was always alone though he liked to talk with his mother. When he came home from work, he would tell his mother all that happened in his office; he also loved his job very much.

Gave birth to Lena

In the ninth month, I was put to bed and Lena was born. Stefan's father came with his sister to visit me in the hospital; as he was coming, he brought the save book and wrote Lena's name on it; he was very happy. I spent about one week in the hospital before Stefan came to take us home after we were discharged. When we got home, I was expecting Stefan to say he would give the child up for adoption, but he never mentioned it again. The neighbours came to visit me and brought presents just to see if the baby was white or black.

Gradually, Lena was growing. When she reached a year and six months, she gradually started walking. I didn't know that she was entitled to some money paid by the German government to any child born in Germany, which was supposed to be given to the mother, especially if she was not working. The father was collecting the money without telling me because he knew I couldn't speak German or understand the language very well.

When Lena was about three years old, Stefan arranged how we would visit Nigeria. He bought the tickets so we could visit Nigeria before Lena started kindergarten. We travelled to Nigeria, and my cousin came to wait for us at the airport. We stayed in a hotel in Lagos the first day, then, the next day, he drove us to Benin City. When we got to Benin, we stayed in a hotel, and my sisters, brothers and some family members came to visit us at the hotel; then gradually, I visited them one by one. I brought four big bags full of presents, and I gave some presents and others money after changing the money to naira. I also gave some money to my mother for cooking food and taking care of Kelly. We stayed about three weeks in Nigeria, bought some items to give to friends and Stefan's relatives, and then returned to Germany. When we got home, Stefan's parents were very happy, and I was also very happy; the sister also came to visit. Anytime Emilia came to visit, Stefan's mother would show that she was the boss of me, and Stefan kept saying I should play along because he brought me from Africa, and in Africa we do more hard work than here. I resumed my Dutch and German lessons at Mrs. Ella's house. I took presents to her when I came back from Nigeria, and I was beginning to understand Dutch little by little.

I was still cooking downstairs, and we were still eating together, but if it was Christmas, Stefan's father would give me 1000DM, saying his other grandchildren would come visiting for Christmas. I would cook, clean the whole house, and arrange the place very well. Christmas was always a very beautiful time. On Christmas day, the grandchildren would bring presents for the rest of the family members and me, and when the New Year was over, they would drive back to their city.

Stefan was a tight-fisted and jealous man; he didn't give me money for food, instead, he bought the food items and brought them home. As Lena grew to three years, she was registered in a kindergarten. I took her there only in the mornings because I was not working, though

I have started attending a driving school along with my Dutch classes. Stefan said he was not going to pay for the driving lessons; he said I would not be able to pass the driving test because I didn't understand Dutch so well. So I took up a job with a family friend who used to dress Stefan's mother's hair. She was looking for someone to help her with house cleaning, but the job was very difficult. The woman would bring out all her belongings, very big items, for me to clean, and when I was through, she would pay me immediately. I gathered the money to pay for my driving lessons since my husband was not willing to pay.

There was also a French lady who was the same age as Stefan, whom I knew through my Dutch teacher; she was always encouraging me. She called me at times and spoke English with me, though my husband didn't want me to be speaking with her. I took my first driving test and passed both the English and the one in Dutch; I was so happy. Now I was able to drive; I would drive Stefan's parents and also the sister out any time she came to visit. If Stefan is driving and I see a black man that shakes my hands, he will look at me with his eyes. He loves himself so much, other people do not interest him. I decided to have a girlfriend who lives around because I heard that there was an African lady who was married to a German man. She also has a daughter, and she is from South America; I was very willing to see and talk to her. I called her; I spoke with her in English, and she said it was not long since she married her husband and that she was happy; she promised to try to come and visit me.

One day, she came to visit with her daughter, and I was upstairs. We just talked, she asked me when I came to Germany and that she had heard about me too. She told me she also doesn't have friends in Bexbach where she lived, but she had South African friends in other cities. She said she used to dance tango dance, and that if I liked, I could join her. One day, I also visited her, and she cooked Ecuadorian food for me; I ate it; it was very delicious, and I enjoyed it very much. She also said I could always come and visit her, but I would have to call her first. I said ok but didn't understand why she asked me to always call her first before visiting because, in Africa, we don't call people before visiting them. When you see them face to face, you tell them when you are coming to visit them, and they will wait for you. I didn't say it loud for her to hear; just kept it in my mind, thinking she didn't want me because she was a white woman. She stays very far from me, like a kilometre distance.

One day, Stefan was on the phone. He said a family friend's wife was asking of me, that she was on the phone; I was very happy, we just talked in English a little bit and she dropped. She is a very nice person; she said she would come and visit me, and she asked me who does my hair; I told her one of my church friends, then she sent the hair cream through the post to me. She said if I like, she will come with her husband, pick me up and we will drive to a big city. I told her that since I married Stefan, I have never been to a big city, and she asked me why?

It was a Saturday, and she and her husband drove to my house and picked me up. I was very happy; she asked me if I knew some of the villages around there, and I said no. We got to Saarbrucken, a very beautiful place, and we saw some black people walking around. We asked some if there was an African shop there, and the passerby described it for us, so we went there. Stefan had given me money to buy hair cream, then we went to another store, and I bought shoes for myself while the husband was waiting for us. The wife knew the place very well because they had been coming to Saarbrucken for a while; I was very happy. We drove back, and they dropped me off first before driving home. When I entered the house, I showed Stefan what I bought, and he said they were ok if I liked them. I said I would put them on Sunday for church. On Sunday, I put on the clothes I bought, the shoes and the scarf on my head and we went to the Roman Catholic Church they attend. They all looked at me in church, saying that is Stefan's wife. There is a Christian sister who sings in that same church, and when she saw me, she was surprised. She came to greet me and told me her name was Julia. We drove home together, and after that day, she called me often; at times I also called her. We became close friends, and I go and visit her sometimes after calling to let her know I am coming.

There was a time Stefan's mother said she heard that I was pregnant again, but I was not pregnant, only that I put on more weight. The village people like to gossip; most of the time, they would stretch their heads through the window and watch people going out and coming in to see what was happening in the village. Just a few black people were living in the village at that time.

Lena finished kindergarten and started primary school. Whenever they meet with parents, if Stefan goes, they would ask him if he is her grandfather, and he would sometimes answer them. Living with Stefan was so boring; he didn't go out or take me out, not even to restaurants, not that he was a poor man or didn't have enough money; and even if he didn't, his parents were ok to help him out whenever he was in need, because any time Stefan goes to the shop to buy things for us, he will also buy for his parents – the parents would see the receipt, check it and leave money on the table. I did not ask him why; I just waited to see what would happen. One day, I asked my Christian friend, Julia, why and she told me that it's normal for the parents to do so, and I told her that in Africa, we don't do that.

One day, Stefan's cousin came to visit me, and she asked me if I could swim; I said no because I am afraid of water, but she said I could learn it. She bought swimming pants for me, but she collected the money from Stefan. She bought them and said she would come and take me to the swimming pool. She came; we went along with Julia and Lena. When we got to the swimming pool, she was playing with Lena and asked me to put on the children's swimming hand safe. I put the hand safe on, and then I got into the small swimming pool; it was very shallow, not deep. Then the children from the big swimming pool were looking at me; I didn't know why? So any time they saw me at the store, they would look at me and tell their mother that this lady could not swim.

Stefan was sick; he had asthma, and he didn't have the power to do difficult tasks, though he was on medications.

He was even warned by the doctor not to have the dove for long because of the smell, which is dangerous for his lungs, but he loves caring for them; he said it's his hobby. So at fifty-six years old, the doctor told Stefan to stop taking care of doves because he was Asthmatic.

Stefan doesn't like me going out, and if I call my mother, he will think I am calling another man outside; he doesn't even allow me to greet African people in the street. At times if Julia comes to see me, he will not tell me, and he will not allow anybody to visit me; except if I am at home, I will open the door for the visitor. When he gave me money for shopping, the money was always a very small amount. I think he was jealous because he was older than me.

He would if he died, I could have everything I wanted; I wouldn't need to work, and there would be enough food, but his father said I must work for future purposes so that when I am old, I will not remain in rent. Stefan's father always encouraged me to do something, to work now so I would not suffer in the future. I heed Stefan's father's advice, so when Lena started school, I would look through newspapers for job vacancies. I saw a job vacancy in the newspaper and called our family friend's wife; she helped me to call them, and they invited me for an interview. When I got there, the lady showed me the room; she looked rich, and they owned the company. We talked about how many times I would be coming and how much I would be paid. We agreed on an amount equivalent to 400 bases today, and then she employed me. When I got home, I told Stefan and his parents, and they said it was ok, though Stefan was really happy about it.

I started work at Zenus, and I would be going three times a week. The first day, she showed me places I would clean, and she also helped me and tried to understand me. She had a big dog I was afraid of, though after a while, I tried touching him. One day Mrs. Zenus bought flowers and gave them to me, beautiful flowers, and I was wondering why she was giving me flowers; she should have given me a little money, not flowers. I gave them to Stefan's mother because they were like leaves to me, and she gladly accepted them.

I continued my Dutch lessons, and one day Mrs. Ella asked me if I could write and understand very well now; I said yes. She asked me for my transcript certificate from Nigeria, Africa, and she said she would help me to translate it and see what would come out of it. So I went home and brought the certificate to her; she translated it and sent it to the ministry in Deutschland and said I should wait; if it's good, then I could go to school in Deutschland to study. I was very happy. I waited for almost three months with no reply. After a while, it came; it was posted to me, and I took it to her. She looked at it and said it was good, that I could stay in Germany if I wanted to. I went home and told the family, and I decided to start the training in an old people's home in Bexbach. I was there for almost two months, and they wanted me to start working there. I said no because my daughter was still very small, so I left.

Later, I started at a nursing school, and after about one year, I decided to go and work in a small clinic nearby. The next day, I went to one of the nurses who had been working there for a long time; I was not perfect in Dutch, so she came along with me to one of the patient's rooms. When we got there, the woman had stool (bowel movement problems). I asked the nurse why the woman was putting on pampas, saying that it's not so in Africa, but she said it's normal. I was just wondering, although I have seen Stefan's father urinating in a bottle while this woman had stool problems. After two weeks, I still could not understand her because it really surprised me. I worked there for about a year and decided to leave; the people there loved me, and one of the patients even bought me a present before he died; I still have the gift to this date.

I left there because the pay was very small; I was just an auxiliary nurse. I went to another place. In my new place of work, some of the nurses were very nice, especially nurse Lea; I became friends with her. Though she had been working there for a long time, she didn't have an educational qualification, but she could work and clean. One of the nurses who also has been there for a long time and was well educated was using her bare hands to remove bowel movements from the anus (without hand gloves). One day I asked her why and she said it works better that way. When we were on break, we would wash the patient's clothes with cold water, rinse them and then put them in the machine. The owners of the old people's home have a house in Spain, and the wife used to tell us that if we wanted to spend our holiday in Spain, we could travel to her place. It was their family business. I was working there with no educational certificate in nursing; I worked from 7am till 2pm, while the afternoon duty was from 2pm to 9pm.

After a while, I started having problems with Stefan; he became more jealous than before, and he kept thinking I had a boyfriend, that even Lena had a boyfriend. I reported him to his doctor; maybe they would be able to help him psychologically. He went to see the doctor but came back almost immediately, so I decided to give him a chance.

Stefan's father became sick. Someone from the state came to investigate the situation, and Stefan's sister also came around; I didn't know what was going on, but I was the person helping Stefan's father; I would clean him up in the morning and the evening, give him his medications morning, evening, and at night as well. He was very ill, and the doctor said he was not going to live long, that he was going to die. Before the investigator came, Stefan's sister told me to go out and visit my friend Julia, so I went to visit her just that day. I didn't know that someone was coming to investigate for the government to be paying the person taking care of Stefan's father. I was taking care of him because he was a nice man, and he was giving me 200DM. After the investigator left, they started paying the money to Stefan's sister.

One day, the investigator came unexpectedly; I was at home, and the woman called me and asked how he was doing. I said he was doing good, and the woman said she was asking me because they were paying money for his care; I then understood. Then Stefan's mother called Emilia on the phone to come immediately, and Stefan went to pick her up. She came and asked the investigator why she didn't call her before coming. The woman told her she had the right to come any time she wanted. While that was going on, Stefan was looking for a way to distract me; he called me upstairs so I would not understand what was going on, and then the investigator left. I went downstairs and asked them if they felt I didn't understand what was going on and told them I was not a fool – I still continued to help Stefan's father.

Then, when it was Christmas time, Stefan's mother gave me the money, adding it to housekeeping money. I told her I would not take the money, and that it was ok. She asked why, and I said because all this while I had been doing this job, helping her husband, they had been the ones collecting the money from the insurance company. She pleaded with me to please forgive her, that it was her daughter who asked her to do so. I had to forgive her, but I was still angry in my heart; I just had to keep laughing because my papers were not yet complete. Though Stefan had done it, it was yet to come out. Stefan also asked his lawyer to write a will so I would not get anything if I left him. So I thought about it, wondering where I would go and where I could start my life. I just had to live with him, though he was a very selfish person.

I left Stefan

After leaving the last old people's home I worked at, I looked for another old people's home and another nursing school. Before I started at the school, I went to the place I had worked before, Zenus, to see a man who told me that any time I had a problem, I should come to him for help because I didn't want to live with Stefan any more. I called him and explained to him, and he said ok, that he would show me how I would start. First, he went with me to Caritas and explained everything to them; they told me to get a house of my own so that I could leave. I got a house and took Lena with me, but she was not happy because she kept on calling for her papa, but the house we lived in was not very far from Stefan's. I was still working in the old people's home. I would leave for work in the morning, and I would leave Lena with my good neighbour; at times, I would ask her if she wished to go and stay with her father while I was at work. Also, Stefan would come around to visit, and we became good friends later on.

After a while, I heard that Stefan's mother had died. We went for the burial ceremony, and after that I started visiting Stefan again, helping him to clean the house. Before I started my new job, I asked him if he was going to help in case Lena needed to come and spend the night with him, and he said no problem. Lena was almost ten years old now; my good neighbours had two daughters around that used to play with her, and their parents and I used to do things together.

There was a friend of mine who was living very far from me, whom I had helped previously. She told me she had a brother in Japan and asked if I would like to travel there; I was still very naïve then. The black man called me on the phone, and we chatted; at this time, Stefan and I were already divorced. After six months, the lady brought me two pictures of her brother and said they had the same father and mother. So I decided to travel to Japan to see him; I checked the cost of the ticket because I did not have enough money. Before I travelled, I prepared everything; it was the holidays; I told Lena and Stefan that I would be travelling and would return after one week. I also told my lady friend to tell the brother that I was coming to see him. I travelled to her place first so she could make my hair; I thought she was a good lady.

Visited Japan

When I left her place, I travelled to Japan, and when I got there, the man came to welcome me; he took me to a hotel. When we got to the hotel, I brought out the two pictures I had brought along with me and showed them to him. When he saw the pictures, one of the photos was him while the other photo wasn't. I was very surprised.

The man said, "Maybe my half-sister sent you to me to test me that she has introduced me to him before."

Then I asked if she was his half-sister, and he said yes, but that was not what she told me. He took me out and bought me a lot of things, a present for Lena and also for his half-sister who introduced me to him. We discussed a lot of things; he tried to understand me, though we did not sleep together. He showed me where he was working and where he lived. He told me he wasn't happy in Japan and that he would just spend some years there and then go back to Nigeria.

He tried to call my senior brother just to know why I left Stefan. I didn't have much contact with my senior brother because he was angry with me for leaving Stefan, saying Stefan was the one that brought me from Africa to Europe, and that is why I should remain with him. All through the time I was living with Stefan, my senior brother never visited or called me; I was the one calling him and asking after his welfare and that of his family, because he never wanted me to come to Europe.

I tried to make him understand so many things, but the man said he could not be my friend, so I decided to travel back to Germany. Immediately I got home, I called the lady friend that introduced me to the black man. I did not tell her what she did; I only asked her who the tall man in the second photo was. She told me his name was Raymond, and he was her brother. I asked if she could give me his phone number; she said yes, and she gave it to me.

Met Mr. Raymond

I called Mr. Raymond, and he came to Bexbach, to the house where I was living, and then I explained to him the reasons I was no longer living with Stefan. He then told me that the reason he was asking was that he doesn't have a wife, but he has two children in Africa. He said he works at UPS Company in Germany.

He left and promised to return; I prepared food and waited for him when he told me he was coming. He came and then told me where he came from in Benin City, Nigeria. He said both his parents were dead and that the mother had only male children, and we just laughed about it. I found him handsome, just like the other man in Japan, though that one was short; he also had a good heart. After the second visit, Mr. Raymond started visiting me frequently; at times, once a month or every two weeks, he would drive down. He used to come alone, claiming that he loved me. We carried on like that for some time.

One day I called him, and I heard a lady's voice on the other end of the phone, and when I asked him who the lady was, he said she was his former girlfriend; that week he did not come. I told Lena that I was travelling, but I did not tell Raymond that I was coming; I just decided to drive down there, and I took Lena to her father's place. I drove down to North Rhine-Westphalia to see him. It was difficult for me to drive down there because it was my first time driving to NRW; there was no navigation, just a map. I got there in the evening, and I had started the journey at 10am that morning. He did not believe me when I called and told him that I was in the area; he was so shocked when he saw me, and he said I came to check on him without informing him because I thought he was hiding a woman in his house; he said he didn't have time for such things.

I went back home the next day because I couldn't drive back that same day. He seemed like a good man, and he said he would introduce me to his ex-wife. So he went to visit her, and while he was there, he called me and asked me to speak with his ex-wife, Marilyn. She came on the line and said she was happy that it was me that the ex-husband found and that she thought he was going to marry an uneducated woman. She was proud of him for having found an educated woman like me because, at that time, I was in Nursing school.

One day, Marilyn came to visit me in Bexbach; she was always smoking and drinking. She also couldn't cook; she said it was Raymond that used to help her out with cooking and cleaning. She said I should not marry him because he gambles, though he is a good man, and truly, as she said, I saw Raymond gambling in one small shop in a nearby village in Homburg. When we got home, I warned him never to gamble again because it's not good, and he said ok. Marylyn was still around then, I told her, and she said he had been gambling for a long time. I told Raymond that if I saw him gambling again, I would leave him. Marylyn told me not to leave him because he was gambling and that he thinks like a child. Marylyn spent one week with me and went back to Dusseldorf; while she was with me, I took her out; she liked African foods and ate whatever I cooked.

Raymond was still visiting me often, then one day, I discovered I was pregnant. I was in my second year in nursing school; before then, I used to clean in an Autopark house. I had been doing that for a long time, just to get enough money to send home and take care of myself. When Raymond came around to my house, I told him I was pregnant by him, and he was very happy. I also told him that since he did not have a good job in Milhew, he should relocate to Saarland and look for a job. He said ok, and I helped him look for a job in the newspapers; I called him to come to Saarland and start the job. He came, and I took him to the man in charge of the job. Later he said he would not take the job, I was surprised, and I wondered if it was because I was naive or because I was in love. I said that I thought he was relocating to where I was so he could also be helping me out, especially now that I was pregnant and also going to nursing school. I couldn't think of a tangible reason he declined the job offer.

I have to wake up very early in the morning to meet up for work. Lena was almost eleven years old now, and she understood that I was pregnant, but Raymond was still in Mulheim and Saarland, spending time here and there. I spoke to one of my classmates in school, Derby; I asked her if she could come to pick me up from my house to school, at least to ease my stress. She agreed, and I was very happy.

Gave birth to Karl

I worked in this condition for some months and then put to bed a bouncing baby boy. The school called me, and my teachers asked me if I would like to wait for one year before going back; I told them I would think about it. I thought about it and decided to stay home for only six months so I could join my mates to sit the exams. Raymond did not want to come to Saarland to stay with me so both of us could take care of the child. I was going to school, working at the auto company, and taking care of the house and Lena.

Some months after I gave birth, Raymond was still in NRW. I called one of my girlfriends that I knew when I was still married to Stefan, though Stefan would not allow her to come and visit me, so I used to go to her house and visit her and her boyfriend; they were not married, but they were living together like husband and wife. She did not live in Bexbach, but she was born there. I called her to come and take over my job in the Auto Company because it was becoming difficult for me to cope with the situation. I explained my situation to the Company Director; she was a very nice woman, and it was from the company I bought my second car. She understood and accepted my friend. When it was time for me to go back to school, I would drive to a friend's place, who lived a long way from me, and would leave as early as 3am to go and pick her up so she could come and take care of Karl while I was at school.

One day, a man came with a form for me to fill out, I did this, and he told me how much I would be getting on be-half of my son Karl, so I spoke with Stefan's sister to ask if she would take care of Karl and collect the money, she agreed because the social man was paying the money into my account so that if I got someone to look after Karl, I would use the money to pay them. After one year and two months, Karl needed to start kindergarten; Stefan was also aware of it and promised to help me, too. Also, my girlfriend Julia's husband was helping, though I had to give him money for fuel. I was doing that because Julia's husband was already a pensioner, and Julia was new-ly divorced from him; he needed someone to be talking to. I encouraged Julia to go back to him because he was a good man. At least he was better than Stefan; he was more caring and used to give Julia money – up to 600DM, according to her. So I spoke to him about Karl, and he agreed to help. Karl still had Stefan's surname because Raymond was yet to prove that he was the father. I need-ed Julia's husband's help, so he came and brought some papers for me to sign. He encouraged me; there were so many forms to fill out, but he helped me and filled them out. Stefan was also getting something out of the fuel money because he came to visit when I needed his help. If I had any issues or questions, I would call him, and he would come and explain things to me. If I finished school early, I would go and pick Karl up from school. He was a quiet boy; he didn't cry much – it was as if he knew the father was not around to help me.

Lost my sister Martha

I was preparing to sit my nursing exams in September when I lost my younger sister Martha. I was in great shock, and I didn't know what to do. I couldn't fly to Nigeria because I didn't have enough money; I was just downcast. Stefan and Julia's family members were around to console me. My school advised me to try to go to school so I could sit my exams. I managed to do the exams though it was very difficult for me to concentrate because I was crying every day, thinking about my sister Martha. She was pregnant with a child, and both she and the baby died. The doctor advised me to stop thinking about her and also to think about myself. Raymond was still living in NRW, and after a week, he came to sympathise with me. After a while, I just had to accept the situation, believing things would work out well one day. But things were not going well at all. I sat my exams and failed them, and they asked me to repeat them in six months. The school gave me some money for my expenses, but it was not enough because I was living in a three-bedroom flat, so I had to manage the money I had. I wasn't able to send money home during that period. I thought about my life and looked up and down. There was nothing I could say; life was really hard.

Six months later, I resat my exams and, by the grace of God, I passed them. I was very happy, so I started looking for a job in Saarland. I wrote many applications, but no hospital wanted to take me. Then, Raymond told me that they were looking for nurses in Mulheim, so I asked Lena if she would like to move to Mulheim with me, and she said yes immediately. So, I went to Mulheim to survey the place first. After visiting the place and seeing it was ok, I waited till Lena was on holiday. I also went to the social welfare office to see if they could help me with the house rent. When I got to the social welfare office, they asked me a lot of questions: how many children I have, how many rooms I want to rent, etc., and they said that I should not rent rooms that were too expensive. So I went and looked for a house to rent. As Raymond was coming back from the city, he said he saw rooms for rent not far from where he lived; he gave me the contact, and I called the person, and she asked me to come so we could discuss the payments. I went to see the woman; we discussed everything, and she showed me the rooms. It was an old house, so I told her I would think about it, and I went back to Saarland, Bexbach, still looking for a job.

After a while, I called Raymond and told him I would be coming over again to look for a house in NRW. I went there and slept over at Raymond's place. While I was there, I decided to also check if I could get a job, so I went to a nearby clinic along the street; I told them that I was looking for a job, and the chief said ok, that she would take me to the nursing sister who would show me the job function. In the morning, I went with the nursing sister, and we were driving from one house to another. After this, I was tested for the job, and then they gave me a part time appointment letter.

After a week, I went back to Saarland to see my children. I asked Raymond to look for a house for me to rent because he was formally working in Dusseldorf, according to him, because I was finding it very difficult to get a house to rent in Mulheim. I also decided to check the newspapers for job vacancies. I saw one, but it was very far from Mulheim. I called the man, and he told me to come, that one of his co-workers would come and pick me up from the bus station. So I went, waited at the bus station, and the lady came. We went to their office, and when I got there, he asked me a few questions, and then he said he would take me full time. I was very happy; he contacted the office where I was working on a part time basis and informed them that he was going to take me full time, so I started.

The first day was very difficult because I had not driven in a big city before. I was late getting to patients; I didn't know the roads, and there was no navigation; I was only looking at the map. I would get home late most days. Raymond was looking after the children; as he didn't have a job any more, he was helping out with Karl. I was the only person working now. For that week, I asked Raymond if he could drive me to work because I found driving in a big city difficult, and I was new there. I didn't have any friends there, though my friends in Bexbach were still communicating with me and asking after my welfare.

After I had worked for some time and gotten my appointment letter, I decided to go back to Saarland, Bexbach and pack my things. Raymond and one of his friends went with us to pack, and when we got there, we packed the things we could, returned to NRW and arranged the things little by little.

The house owner was not German; she understood me and was nice. At first, if she cooked, she would give me some, and we would sit together in the sitting room and discuss things together, but later she became a bad person; she wrote a petition against Raymond because he didn't support her in court to witness against one of the tenants who she said insulted her. He told the truth about what really happened, so she became very angry and asked us to leave her house. I went to social housing to look for another flat, which they gave me immediately because I was working. We had to pack again, and we moved into the new flat; I didn't renovate this one because it was very beautiful and expensive. I was working a full time job and also working in 400 Base just for me to be able to pay all my insurance fees, buy food and all other things I had been paying in Deutschland. Raymond secretly kept on gambling; I saw some of the gambling papers around the cupboard and wardrobe, and I called him several times to change his lifestyle.

I was now urgently looking for a job that paid better while still working at 400 Base. I got another job at Rhienhouse; it was ok; they started me on very low wages, and I was still working at the old people's home. I had to tell them at Rhienhouse that my flat is big and expensive so that they would add to my salary. Stefan was paying the children's fees, about 220 euros, and I didn't report him to social welfare that the money he was giving was not enough because Stefan thought I didn't know how much he was supposed to give me for child benefit. I reasoned that if Raymond could not cater for his own child, why should I ask Stefan to pay me more money?

I kept managing my income, but Raymond would still go out and visit friends in the evening; if he saw that I was not home, he would go out and gamble. I often had to advise him to change his behaviour, that if he sent that money to his mother at home, she would be happy. I had not met the mother, but sometimes I bought things like African fabrics and sent them along with vitamin tablets to her. Then I was doing all these things because I felt I was blinded by love, but I was beginning to see he could not change; we fought each other. He would use abusive words on me, disgrace me, and then I would call the police on him.

After some months, my brother, who lived in Italy, asked me to visit home, so I bought tickets for myself and my son Karl. When I got to Nigeria, I stayed with my brother. Raymond later came to Nigeria, and he wanted to stay with me at my brother's house. I refused, so he stayed in his family's house. After some days, I went to visit Raymond's family. They all welcomed me, and when they saw Karl, they were very happy. I told Raymond's brother that Raymond was not responsible and that he gambled a lot. Then his brother, who was a very good Christian and the one taking care of Raymond's mother, and his brother's children tried to advise Raymond to stop gambling.

After spending two weeks in Nigeria, I returned to Germany; things were now moving fine for me. I resumed work. Raymond was yet to get a job, but he was hardly ever home. Anytime I came back from work, I would call him to find out where he was and if he had gone gambling again or gone to his friend's place instead of staying home and looking after his son. I tried to find a job for him but couldn't find one. Then we fought again, and I called the police. He took my car keys and was shouting; the police came and asked him to leave the house for some days, which he did. Later, he asked his friend to come and beg me to allow him back in.

After a while, I realised I could no longer afford the house rent. I had no other option but to quit the house and look for something smaller. Any house I saw, Raymond would say was not beautiful enough; I didn't listen to him because I was looking for one I could afford. Then I saw one, the flat was very small, and the rent was also low; I could afford it without asking for help from the government. I rented a bus and moved my things to the new place. At this time, my daughter Lena had finished school; she was working in another state and no longer staying with me.

After moving to the small flat, Raymond brought his two sons from Africa. I didn't know he was working on their papers, although I knew at the beginning, but I thought he had stopped working on them. He called me one day and said his two sons had gotten visas to come to Germany. I was surprised; I asked him how he did it, and he said when he sat for his lorry driving license when he started work at one of the companies in Mulheim, he added some papers they would need from the company at the embassy. He said he needed to bring his sons to Germany because it would make his life better, and also the children kept saying he was not doing enough for them, that his mates abroad had a lot of landed properties in Nigeria, and their families were living well.

So he pleaded with me to help them learn the Deutsch language. He took them to the school; they admitted them, and the school gave them the date they would start, so I took them to the shoe shop and bought shoes and clothes for them. At the shops, the children were busy looking at expensive shoes and clothes; I ignored them and decided to buy them the ones I could afford because their father had started working three months before this. I thank God he finally got a job because he had been without a job for too long, and it was causing quarrels every day at home.

Living with Raymond and his two children

When Raymond finally started working again, and his two children from Nigeria joined us in Germany, we looked for a bigger house, bigger than the one we were living in before. It was an up and down flat with rooms upstairs and downstairs. His children were living upstairs while we were living downstairs with Karl. Karl's room was small, but it was ok for him; he was now in primary school. Raymond's children started giving me problems though they were still going to school. I tried to show them love, but they were not reciprocating it to me. They were over eighteen years old, and they wanted big things. They made a lot of friends, even girlfriends. They were keeping late nights, and they were full of lies. I told their father to look for another house for them; their father had lost his job because he had an accident, and he was also sick with high blood pressure, heart problems and many other ailments. He wanted his children to remain with me; I told him no, that the children were big enough to stay on their own, but Raymond was still insisting that they should stay with us.

By now, the love between us was diminishing, so he went and rented a one-room apartment for them, but he was still living with us. We had issues every day. The children's mother in Nigeria never once called me to thank me for taking care of her children, maybe she thought I took her man from her, but I was carrying almost all of the burden in the house, taking care of her children, paying the house rent, insurance and some other bills. When Karl started seeing how they were behaving, he started losing concentration. The teacher called me one day from school, saying that Karl was not concentrating in school. I felt really bad and told Raymond that it would be better if the children moved to the room he rented for them, but he was still insisting, and the children did not want to leave; they kept giving me problems, fighting with their father and destroying things in the house, so I called the police, and the police asked them to leave my flat, after all, they were not registered occupants in the flat.

Their father still did not want to understand, so I asked him to leave also. He started begging me, but since I didn't love him any more, I insisted he must leave, so he decided to pack his things and go. Before he left, he beat me up and wounded me on my face; Karl was shouting; if Karl had not been there, maybe he would have killed me. I called the police; the police came and warned him not to come within a certain distance of me again. He started begging me, and he sent some of his friends and relatives to come and beg me, saying that he beat me because I did not accept his other children.

My mother's visit to Germany

I invited my mother to visit me in Germany, and when she came, she was also begging me to please forgive and understand Raymond; I said no. After some months, my mother went back to Nigeria. I allowed him to come in before my mother left because I had to respect my mother's wishes so she would not feel bad. My friends who came to visit my mother advised him to change, so I forgot about my issues with him for some time, thinking maybe he would change, but he was still insisting that the children should come back. We exchanged words, and he beat me up again. He put his leg on my head, and I started shouting for help. Karl, too was shouting and crying that he should leave me alone, but he refused. I finally was able to loosen his grip on me, and I ran out and called the police. I told the police that I didn't ever want him to stay with me again, that he should pack his things and leave my flat. It was then I realised that if I continued with Raymond, he would kill me one day. I didn't want to leave him because people would laugh at me, especially my relatives, but I just couldn't take the beatings any more, so he packed his things and finally left my flat.

Meeting Felix

After some years, a Nigerian lady whom I knew in Bexbach called me to say that she was coming to visit me; she came with her husband and children. When she came, we discussed it, and she introduced me to her brother, who lives in Italy; she said the brother was a very good, responsible and hard-working man. I asked her questions about her brother, how many children he had, if he was married and other necessary questions. She said he was not married, but he had five children. After a few days' visit, she left with her family, and two weeks later, her brother, Felix, came to Germany to visit me; he looked innocent and nice.

As he was coming, he bought some things for me; he had already asked his sister about the sizes of my underwear. I was so impressed because Raymond never bought anything for me. I was the one doing everything. I did not invite him to my flat; instead, I booked a room away from my flat, where we both went to talk. I asked him more questions, but I still did not agree to his advances because he had many children. He spent two days and went back to Italy. When he left, I felt he was a nice man, and he was somebody I would like to live with and marry. He came again the second time to visit me; he was doing a lot of things for me, and he sure knew how to influence a woman. I also tested him in so many ways. He was ok, and the way he talked and understood the situation, he looked like a responsible man.

When he came the third time to visit me, I had already bought a flat, so he helped me to pack and move. When we moved to the new flat, we celebrated the achievement by inviting some friends and relatives. He was so helpful, like a man I really needed, and I fell in love with him. I was now taking good care of my body; he taught me how to cook and so many other things. If I said something was wrong, he would correct me gently; if I wore a dress, he would say whether it was ok or not; he was very understanding.

Married again

I was also the one working and spending my money because he also didn't have a job, but he promised me that if he got a job, he would assist me in paying for the mortgage on the flat. All this made me feel he was a nice man, and he was someone I could spend the rest of my life with. I didn't care about what I was spending on him.

After being together for a while, he told me he was planning to travel to Nigeria. I told him to hold on, and the sister insisted we get married, so he brought the marriage papers to Germany, and I took them to the marriage registry for verification. They said they were going to investigate if he was married and if the marriage papers he brought were correct. When I got home, I told him everything they had said, and he said I should not worry; even the sister said I should not be worried and that the brother was a nice man, and that he would treat me well. She advised that we go to Denmark to get married, so I called the Denmark registry. I told them we wanted to come and get married there and that we would send them the papers for the marriage; they said ok, and we started planning for the marriage.

I had to rent the hotel room we were going to stay in for one week before the marriage. In this hotel, we had to cook for ourselves, and I did not have enough money in the bank. We managed to get married there; we left my car at the train station and took a train to Denmark. We had to buy food and other needed items from the shops, and things were very expensive in Denmark. I just bought the cheap items, and when we got to the hotel, I prepared them. I noticed one thing about him that very day when we were buying things in Denmark; he picked a shirt for himself. I told him I didn't have enough money, so I couldn't buy it, and he got very angry. He thought I had a lot of money and was very rich; then I realised that I had made another very big mistake concerning men, but I had already made arrangements for the marriage.

I invited the sister, but she didn't come. She said she didn't have the money to travel down. We went ahead with the marriage; he brought the rings he came with from Italy because he wanted us to get married immediately. We got married and put the rings on our fingers. When we were through, Felix said he could not wear the ring because he had surgery on his ring finger; I was just looking at him. We left Denmark the next day, took a train, and returned to the train station to pick up my car. I got there and saw that they had put a paper on the car, and that I had to pay for parking in the wrong place. When we got home, I registered him in the registry that we were now married.

I resumed my work. At times, I was on night duty. Then one day, one of the ladies that I invited to my flat when I celebrated buying the house called me, saying it's a pity that I married Felix, that she knows me very well, that I am a good person but that Felix is a useless man, that he is not a responsible man at all. She said she had been thinking about whether to tell me or not. I told her no problem and that she could tell me anything. The lady said that immediately I left for work, Felix would be calling her for a date and that he had fallen in love with her; she said she could no longer keep quiet about it, which is why she was telling me. I said to myself that if I had known the kind of man he was, I wouldn't have married him.

Later on, one of my cousins who lived in Italy also called me on the phone and said she had something to tell me. She said when she came to visit me, that my husband gave her a dress and some money to give to a lady who also lives in Italy. The dress was for a girl of about five to six years old. I asked Felix about what my cousin said. That was when he started telling me that there was a lady in Italy who had a baby girl by him. I asked him why did he had not told me before now, and he said he was afraid that I would not marry him if I knew. I said that from the onset I told him I needed someone who would always tell me the truth; he didn't tell me at first, and even his sister did not tell me. I was angry that I had fallen victim again. I called the sister, and she claimed that she herself was not aware. I decided not to mind, as long as the lady was not living in Deutschland and not only that, he was also not married to her.

After a while, he became eager to travel to Nigeria, so I bought a ticket for him, and he went. When he got to Nigeria, I called him, but he did not reply, so I called his son, who he had introduced me to before. The boy told me his father had a problem with his mother in Nigeria. I asked him if he could give me his mother's number, and he did, and I called her. I greeted her and asked her what the problem was. She told me she has seven children with Felix, and now the family wants her to separate from him and leave his house. I was shocked; it was as if the phone would fall from my hand. I said this man did not tell me who he really was. Even Raymond was much better than him. Felix was full of lies. I cried my eyes out. I could not explain it to anybody, and I wished I had called Raymond back.

Felix kept on womanising, even though he didn't have a fixed job; he had never worked in any place for long, not to talk of having any appointment letters. I really regretted marrying him. I was the one paying the bills, and there was no help from him; I used to drop him at school, but when I saw that the burden was heavy on me, I asked him to start going to school by himself. I bought him tickets and showed him twice how to get to the train station to Mulheim and back. I did that for about three months without help from the state. He did the exam for the first time and failed. He had to stop school, and he stayed at home for some months. I told him he had to go to school and learn the language for him to be able to get a good job. He later got approval, so he started going for lessons; he sat the exams the second time and passed. I told him to continue with the school so he could have a B[1]. He said he didn't come to Germany just to go to school; he had a family to feed, and he is already getting old, so he stopped at a[1] and got a gardener's job instead, but he still had some problems because his Dutch and German was still not good. There were two of them working in the garden, but after working for nine months, they sacked them; he couldn't explain why. I had to help him look for another job. He got another job as a helper in a restaurant; they were able to manage him because he changed his character a bit. They used to send him on errands, and when he got home, he complained that they kept sending him here and there. I reminded him that I advised him to continue with school so he could get a befitting job, but he refused to take my advice. After a few months of working there, he was sacked again.

One day, he got drunk, insulted me, calling me all sorts of names; rubbish came from his mouth, and I cried and blamed myself for marrying such a man. It had been three years now since we got married, and he was bringing out all his bad characteristics. I called the sister who introduced him to me and reported everything to her; she apologised for everything the brother was doing to me and promised to talk to him. She spoke with him, saying that he should stop drinking. I was ashamed of myself because I knew that the people that knew us would be laughing at me. I started thinking of many things, and I was afraid I might even lose my house. Then all I had paid would go to waste. I thought of the right thing to do, and I decided to call the Mortgage Company; they gave me an appointment to come, though I wrote a letter first and paid. I met with them, and later they sent me the original papers. I then relaxed myself, Felix also calmed down a bit, and we were living a little happier together, although, in my heart, I didn't love him any more. Whenever he was on call, he would go outside the bedroom to talk to the person so I would not hear what they were saying. I didn't care; after all, I am not always at home.

One day, I called him and asked him to sit down. I told him to try to think of other things to do; he can learn Deutsch through YouTube and also get a good job and make good friends online, and not just be talking and talking on the phone, saying what he is not supposed to say or pretending to be who he is not because henceforth, he would not get any help from me. He should work hard for himself. If he wants to travel to Nigeria, he should use his money to cater for all expenses, because I heard he was planning to travel to Nigeria soon. He bought a bus for himself when he was still working as a gardener; he was just using me, thinking I was a fool. I just looked at him and laughed, saying to myself that he was more foolish than I was because he was going to leave my house soon.

After a while, when I saw that he was jobless again and his character was better, I told him I would go to the bank and borrow money for him to start an importation business, buying old used cars to sell in Nigeria because he used to brag that when he was in Nigeria, he was in an importation business. I went to the bank and borrowed about 20,000 euros for him, but I warned him seriously not to mess up this time around. I checked the newspapers and saw some lorries for sale, so I called them. I also asked one of my friends, a black man, to help him with the business, so he came with us to buy the lorry. When we got there, Felix was misbehaving with the dealers, talking as if the money was his; even the people that went with us behaved themselves. We bought the lorry and drove home, and it was parked where he was going to load it. He had some items he picked from the roadside and some used clothes that he kept. So he arranged for them to be put in the lorry.

Anytime he went to where the lorry was being loaded, he would dress fine, and anybody that saw him would think he had money, whereas there was nothing in his pockets. I usually asked him why he was dressing like that, that couldn't he wear working clothes like the people working there, but because he was so proud, he would not listen. I told him that even in the bible, God says we should not be proud.

After two weeks, we bought another lorry to join the other one. I also gave him the car I was driving before, along with other items, and he took them to Nigeria; we had to pay the loaders and the transport company out of the money I borrowed too. All this I did for him, yet he was still womanising despite the warnings I gave to him. When he got to Nigeria, he stayed first in a hotel in Lagos for some days to clear the goods. The clearance money became very high because of the devaluation of the Nigeria Naira, so I had to send money to my junior brother to help out with the situation because he didn't have any money, not even in Nigeria; I was the one helping his entire family. I advised him to sell off everything in Lagos, but he refused and carried them to Benin City because he wanted to show off, for people to know that he had been in Germany and that he had money, especially his friends in Benin.

After selling the items he brought to Nigeria, he left a small amount of the money with my junior brother and started planning to buy a house. I asked how much he had sold all the items for, and he said he had not sold most of the items. I told him I hoped he knew I borrowed the money we used for this business from the bank and that I had to pay back the money gradually, but he did not listen. I told him he had to send me 2000 euros immediately to send to the bank where I took the money, but he didn't. I now had to tell my younger brother to send me 1000 euros from the one with him, so I could give it to the bank, or else I would be in trouble. It was 5000 euros that were with him.

My husband would buy a car and take it to Nigeria to sell, but because he had plenty of children and a lot of expenses to meet, he would spend the money and still request my brother give him more from my money. I had to tell my brother not to give him money again because he was wasting it on frivolities. The third time he went on a business trip to Africa, I told him to save money for whatever he wanted to buy because he would never get any of my own money again. He saved money for about one and a half years. I didn't know how much he was able to save, but he was able to buy some cars to take to Africa without touching my money.

I was now working in one of the villages in Germany, going with other nurses from house to house to attend to patients. One day, I went with one of the nursing sisters to see a patient named Vicky; we were to clean her up, but Vicky said no, and the sister asked her why. She said she had never seen a black lady before; the sister started laughing, saying there were many black people in Deutschland now, and sister Mercy was not too black. I just kept quiet and was looking at the woman. I told the sister to clean her up by herself. She was angry and said that could not be, that she needs to learn to like other people and other nursing students also. Vicky did not say anything, the white nurse cleaned her up and we left, but the next day we still had to go there and clean her up again and give her medications.

When we got there the next day, while still in the car, I told the nursing sister that I didn't think Vicky would allow me to clean her up; rather, I should stay in the car, and she go inside alone. She told me not to worry and that she would talk to Vicky, so we went inside and cleaned her up. We worked with some other patients without any problems; some of them even liked me. Still, one of the patients wanted to be problematic, then the sister told her if she didn't allow me to clean her up, we would not come again, and her appointment would be cancelled; she got the message and allowed me to clean her up. I followed the sister to attend to the patients for one week; Sunday was the last day I was to finish with them, and when I got there, Vicky apologised for her behaviour on the first day, and I told her it was ok.

After the practicals, I started working there. My chief's mother was also brought to the old people's home, and we were taking care of her; she was blind. They would send me to clean her and give her food. The first time I saw her, she was shouting hello every minute; I took her and sat her between two old people, yet she still shouted hello; I thought I was going to develop hearing problems because of her shouts. The other nurses didn't like to go and attend to her; when they saw that I was new, they would ask me to go and attend to her and any other difficult old patients.

My son Karl was living with me, and I didn't have enough money to attend to my needs. The government support was small because I was now married; if I wanted more support from the government, I would have to apply. Raymond, Karl's father, was not supporting him at all, even though he was working at that time and even had a girlfriend. Karl told me when he went to visit him that he was happy for his father now that he had a girlfriend to keep him company. I replied that I was also happy for him. Whenever Karl went to visit his father's place, the father did not give him any money, not even as small as 20 or 10 euros. Sometimes three months would pass without him calling to ask about the welfare of his son. I would call and quarrel with him, at times trying to force him to come and pick Karl up, but he would still not come, but if it was a party Karl was to attend, he would come because he loves partying and friends.

Death of Raymond

Karl's father, Raymond, was still living with his children he had brought from Nigeria; we were discussing them one day when he came visiting, and he told me that they had been arrested for stealing and that they were imprisoned. He said the younger one was released after six months, but the senior one was still there and that he was going to get a lawyer for him. We discussed some other issues, and after a while, he left and went to his house. A few months later, I was called and told that Raymond was dead, that he died of high blood pressure.

A few days later, I was at work on night duty; Karl was crying at home even though I asked someone to help me care for him. He said he was missing his papa, that even though he didn't give him any money, at least let him be alive because he loved his dad with all his heart. Before Raymond died, he apologised and said he was sorry, but I was already married to Felix. So I comforted Karl and told him I also missed his papa. His friends and church members gave him money for the burial. For Karl, that year was a very painful one. He came to me one day and said, "Mummy, I have a friend who is six years old, and he just lost his father also. I think I am in a better position to encourage him now."

Three days after the burial, Karl and I went to the cemetery where Raymond was buried. When we got there, Karl cried and told me to give him some moments alone, that he wanted to talk to his father; I gave him some space. When he finished, he came to me and said he felt better now, and I told him his father was a good man and that most times, when we are old, we begin to realise and see the mistakes we made when we were younger, that he is still a child, he might not be able to understand now. I told him I had been the only one taking care of him and even his senior brother Kelly, and Kelly also lost his father at a very young age. I told him I had been a single parent for a very long time now, and even when I was with Lena's daddy, he couldn't hold Lena for long because he was much older than me. He was like a father to me because of the age gap, but now Lena is helping a lot; I thank God I am still in Deutschland. I struggled to buy a flat because the whole house cost a lot. I worked so hard in order to be able to pay for the mortgage of the flat. Though I have a husband, it was like I didn't have a husband. Karl told me it was ok; he knew I was doing my best for him and that when he is old enough and gets a good job, he will be helping me out. I told him he didn't need to work hard for me. I have struggled enough for myself, and rather he should work hard for himself, whether he is here in Deutschland or Africa, because life is very difficult, especially for those of us with black skin.

When we got home, he sat down for a while and said that as the father was being buried in the cemetery, a lot of people asked for his address and said they would be coming to ask after him, but as of today, none of them have come, even his father's brother has not come to see him. I told him not to worry; when he grows up and achieves his goals, they will all come one day. I encouraged him because Karl didn't know how to pretend. Later he started playing his games, and when it was night, I went to bed to sleep. The next day he went to school, and I went to my work.

One day, when I got home from work, I was sitting down in the sitting room. Karl came in and asked where his uncle was; he didn't know my husband's name, so he called him uncle. I told him he had gone to bed, then he sat with me and said he didn't understand him, that if I was home, he would go to bed very early, but if I was not at home, he would stay in the sitting room for a very long time. I told Karl not to worry and that Felix could do whatever he wanted to do. If he felt that what he was doing was right, let him continue. I couldn't stay home all day because I wanted to monitor him. After that, Karl went to his room, and I also went to mine. I did not ask Felix about what Karl said; we kept on living like that.

As I was thinking about Felix's issues one day, I told him I would look for another job for him to do along with the business so that he would not have much time to chat on the phone. I have the phone number and e-mail address of the phone company he is currently working for in case they gave him instructions he couldn't understand because of his poor understanding of Deutsch; I would be able to call them and explain to them properly. He said no, that he wanted to go to Africa, and that if he came back, I could do that. So I waited until he returned from Africa. I got a job for him when he came back, where they used to park lorries because he said he needed more money. With all the money he was getting, he still didn't give me any for food or anything. I felt so stupid and angry with myself for marrying him. As we were quarrelling one day, I told him that from that day, he should give me money for food and housekeeping, that if he couldn't afford it, he should leave, look for another house and pay his own house rent, phone bills, food and many other things. He was receiving up to 700 euros, so it wouldn't be so bad if he gave me a minimum of 150 euros; if not, he should leave my house. I told him he was a wicked man, that is why he was not progressing, and that even the bible says a man should provide for his wife and family.

Lost my beloved mother

During this process, I lost my mother. I tried to save some money, so I could buy a ticket and go to Nigeria for the burial rites because according to tradition, if a mother dies, depending on the family she came from, as the first daughter and married, I must be present to do what the family wants me to do. So I prepared, bought a ticket and flew to Nigeria for the burial ceremony. I had to buy a ticket for him also because he said he didn't have money; because according to tradition, he had to be present, whether he had money or not. So I had to do everything allocated to me for the burial ceremony though he kept boasting that he had invited his family and friends.

During the burial proper, the first thing we did was to bring my mother out of the mortuary. He wasn't there, but when we got to my mother's street, I saw him there dancing too. My mother's family was already in the house to receive their sister's remains. He waited for some time in the house and then left. My siblings had already arranged for everything before I got to Nigeria. They made preparations for the food, the church, the venue of the reception and other things; they really helped me a lot. During the social dance, I had to dress according to tradition; as a Bini princess. My friends and family were pinning money on me; my husband did not pin any of his money; instead, he was collecting the money people were pinning and putting it back on me. After the burial ceremony, I spent two weeks and left to go back to Germany.

Missing my mother

I miss my mother and my family in Nigeria, especially my younger brother and sister, who acted so mature-
ly toward me, and I am still very grateful to them for
that today. I remembered my mother when she came
to Germany; it was summer. The first time we talked,
she said the weather was not cold and that when it was
winter, and the weather was cold, she would want to go
back to Africa. She used to tell me what was happening
at home in Africa, about the people I used to know in the
village, the ones that were still alive and the ones that
were dead. My mother was an independent woman who
did not depend on her children. She used to complain
that things were expensive in Africa, but she would not
ask us directly for money.

We used to make fun of her, and she would laugh. She
used to tell us then how she suffered as a young woman,
right from her first husband, whom she gave birth to five
children for, but only two survived. How she had to get
married early and not go to school so that her younger
brother could go to school; because her mother had just
the two of them. The family just called her one day and
presented her to a man she was seeing for the first time
and said as from today, this man is your husband. She
couldn't object, she just went ahead to marry the man.

When she started giving birth, some days after deliv-
ery, the child would die. The husband's family were not

Christians; they were diabolical and made a lot of sacrifices. I told my mother that for me; I didn't believe that it was the sacrifices that were killing her children, that maybe it was infections because in Africa, they didn't maintain proper hygiene and there were no good doctors, and even at that time, some women still delivered babies at home because they didn't have money for hospital bills. If the woman and the child were lucky, they would survive; if they were not lucky, they would die, or one of them would die.

My mother was laughing, and she said I couldn't understand because the world was deep and because I lived in Germany, I should not undermine people. She continued her story and said that after the death of the last child out of the three that died; she left the man and went to marry my father. She said my father was a nice man, but she could not give birth to a male child for him, and he was seriously looking for a male child because he was from a royal family, so he married other women who also gave him female children.

I remembered when my mother took me and my late sister, Martha, to visit my father; when we got there, my father was not at home, so we waited outside. As we were going around, we saw a woman; she was a dwarf, and she was deaf and dumb. We went to call our mother and told her that it was like our father had a new wife. My mother came and tried to talk to the woman, but she couldn't speak, so my mother used her hand to demonstrate to her so she would understand, and she also articulated her response to my mother. It seemed my mother understood her and waited until my father came back; he had a white bicycle. As we saw him coming, we ran to embrace him.

We went into the house, and my mother asked him if he had married again; he said yes, and my mother said it was ok, that this one was young, and maybe she would be able to give him a baby boy. He said yes, of course, and my mother laughed. My mother continued her story and said it was because of my father's cravings for a baby boy that caused his early death. I asked my mother what was so special about having a male child; she said it was very important in Africa, especially as my father was from a royal family. I told her it was not so in Europe, that because of male children, people don't last in Africa.

My mother told me she was very happy I was working very hard in Europe to get to where I am now, that if they had told her before now that Mercy would become a nurse in Europe, she would not believe them. My mother was very happy when she came to Germany; I was still working in the rest house at ambutdienst at that time. I would take a car on loan, and at the end of the month, it would be deducted from my salary, which was ok for me. I was running two shifts, morning and evening; if I was on the evening shift, I normally got home by 10pm; thank God I was mobile. The job was also stressful at the time my mother was around because I had to cook for her, though Karl was able to teach her how to warm the food with the microwave if no one was at home to do it for her. She understood that I had to work because she also loved to work; she was a very hardworking woman from whose lifestyle one can get a lot of wisdom.

Reflecting on my late sister's life

I also thought about my late sister Martha and how she died. I was already working as a nurse at that time with different instruments, and my co-workers were very nice to me. I was very happy living in Germany because since I arrived, I had never experienced a bad co-worker; they were all very nice to me. As a nurse, I helped people a lot and have been able to save a lot of patients, so I feel very bad that I couldn't help my sister when she was sick. I thought about her life in Africa. My sister Martha was living in Lagos, Nigeria, in Africa; she got married, and her life was going well as a young lady because she was educated, and the man she married was also educated; both of them understood themselves, but when she was seven months pregnant, her husband died, and life became difficult for her. I was already in Europe at that time, so I could not go and see her. After the husband's burial, she went back to Lagos, and two months later, she put to bed a baby boy, and he was named Akachukwu.

When Akachi was three months old, my sister had to leave Lagos and move down to Benin City, our home city, because things were becoming very difficult for her in Lagos; there was no help from anyone. At first, she was living with my mother. She looked for a job and started working so she could support my mother with food and also take care of herself and her child. Later, she left my mother's house and rented a room close to her workplace while her son still lived with my mother and younger siblings. I had to support her because there was nothing like social welfare in Africa; the only compensation she got was her husband's gratuity, which she shared between herself and the husband's family. I had to send her money to start a new life because there was no government support or rich family members, and friends were ready to help. We had to pray to God almighty to help us with the situation at that time.

After a while, she continued with her struggles and went back to school to study another course at the University while still working and trading. After nine years of living alone, she met another man and married him, not knowing that the man was still married to his first wife. He lied to my sister that they were already divorced because he was looking for a male child, and he also saw that my sister was very industrious, as at then, she was already building her own house in Africa.

When my sister got pregnant with him, she fell sick and was rushed to the hospital. My youngest sister was the only one taking care of her in the hospital because, at that time, the man was working in another city. They were calling him to come, but he kept giving the excuse that they would not release him from work. After about one week, he came and took my sister to another hospital in his village and left her there, saying he wanted to go and take proper permission from work. He never came back until my sister died with the baby in her womb. He came back, but he didn't pay the hospital bills, I and my siblings in Europe were responsible for all the hospital bill payments and the burial expenses. After the burial of my sister, the new husband ran away with the documents for the house my sister was building before she died, and till today we still have not seen him.

The majority of African men shy away from responsibility; they will abandon the children for the woman to care for all by themselves. Even with such an attitude from African men, the African woman still has to love her husband's family members as well because if she doesn't love them, she will not really have a chance to stay peacefully with the man she married. They will look for any way to destroy the woman, except for those family members who are not expecting anything from her or who are true Christians who understand the bible and fear God.

Also, the government in Africa has no form of assistance for women. In Europe, if you do not have money and you are living alone, you will get help from the government. My sister's son, Akachi, had to return to my mother's house to stay with her. I, as a single parent, was the one sending money to my mother. I couldn't send much; I only sent the little I could afford. My younger brother in Europe also sent money home for my mother, my younger sister, Kelly and Akachi. Akachi's father's family was nowhere to be found; they never cared to even ask after the child, whether he was still alive or not. My mother was already old at that time; she was able to do the little she could by ensuring the boy went to school, ate well and had the important things in life. If not for the mother's family, maybe Akachi would be roaming the streets, and he wouldn't have been able to go to school,

eat or wear good clothes. We had to be calling my mother to talk to and encourage the boy to be good.

When he was through with secondary school, he proceed-
ed to the university, and my younger brother in Europe
was paying his school fees because he was a man who
loved his family very much and he has a fear of God, while
I was helping out with money for food and other petty
things. If it were to be in Europe, the child would get assistance from the government, but in Africa, things are
not like that; things are just so difficult in Africa, especially if the person is not educated.

My last man

My husband came home one day, and I saw that he had been drinking; he smelled of alcohol. He said no, that he didn't drink, so I kept watching him. Another day, before I left for work, I searched his bag and saw a big bottle of whisky; I didn't say anything, and I went to work. When I came home from work, I asked him about the bottle of whisky; he denied it and started insulting me, asking me why I was investigating him, that he was a man so he could do whatever he liked, and that I had no respect for him. He said he didn't go to parties or smoke cigarettes, so he could buy drinks as much as he wanted. I looked at him, and I thanked God that I did not have a child for him; assuming I did, I would have become a single mother to another child again because he was not someone that could care for or love a child, all he did was think about himself. He worked only four to five hours a day, and after that, he did nothing except chat unnecessarily on the phone, calling people in Africa and deceiving them about his true personality. African men know how to hide secrets from their wives; before the woman discovers the truth, many years will have passed.

Some will have a wife in Africa; they will not say it because they want to marry you in Europe to get their papers or because they want to live in Europe. Some of these men are very secretive, just like my husband, Felix. He kept the secret that he was still married to other women from me. He had four wives that had children with him; he told me he had five children, only for me to discover later that he actually had twelve. Some of these African men also have side chicks, they will manipulate the women, and if they catch anyone who doesn't have common sense, she will become their victim. They don't care what happens to the woman; all they care about is sleeping with the woman. Even when you ask questions about them, you will hardly find the truth.

Felix's fourth wife is even living in Europe; he also deceived her because he is still living with this woman in Europe while still living with me. The woman is not aware that he married a fifth wife, which is me and was also living with me. He will tell her that where he is working, the people he is living with will not allow anyone to visit him, and the place is also very small. The woman will only wait to see him whenever he comes to her. I don't have the lady's contact; he keeps hiding to send her small amounts of money, claiming he doesn't have a job and that living in Europe is difficult, telling all sorts of lies here and there.

He always complains about everything; the children are disturbing him to send them money for school fees, etc. I told him not to disturb me with his numerous children's issues because he had never even told me about them before, and he should continue to do whatever he pleases. The most annoying aspect of his character is that if he is hungry, he cannot take food from the freezer and warm it, or if he is at work, take money from his pocket and buy snacks for himself; he will remain hungry or wait till I come back from work to cook and give him food even though he had diabetes. I kept doing all these things for him until one day I told him to drop my keys and ask the personnel officer who issued his name on the post box to remove his name. I told him to pack, get out of my flat and go rent his own house, that I could not continue to cope with his pride any longer and that he should leave, and he said ok. I gave him two months to leave my house, he thought it was easy to live in Europe, and he said he would go and get a social room from the government by seeking political asylum. I told him to go ahead, and I wished him luck. He started packing his things gradually, and finally, after two months, he left my house.

Back to single motherhood

I was very happy when he left. I used other bed sheets on my bed, opened my windows for fresh air to come in, and prepared a very delicious meal to eat: rice, chicken and salad. As I was eating, my son asked me why he left; I told him because he had refused to change for the better. He laughed and said it was better he left, that I should look for a European man to marry or, better still, just have a boyfriend. I told him I didn't want any man in my life again; I didn't want to rush home from work to cook for a man. I wanted to create time for myself; even if I was less busy, I would take a walk or go to the city and look around, just to see the beauty of the city.

My son said ok, that he was grown now, he could take care of himself, and if he needed anything, he would call me on the phone. I wasn't hurrying home any more; I could now call my friends and family members freely, unlike before when he would monitor all my conversations. I could now relax myself, no pimples on my face, my co-workers were even testifying that I looked relaxed. I was afraid to let Felix go before now because I thought that if he left, I would be alone again and people who knew me would laugh at me, but now I realised that it was better to be alone than to die in a relationship or marriage. Life is sweet and very good in Europe if you work hard for yourself.

Today, I am a new person; I went to the salon to make my hair and change the colour, and when I looked at myself in the mirror, I smiled to myself and said I love myself. I am a very hardworking lady, so I used this opportunity to take good care of myself; after all, life is too short to be wallowing in self pity. When I finished at the salon, I went to a small restaurant to eat alone with a very small amount, and I enjoyed it. The woman serving in the restaurant asked me if it was my first time there, and I said yes. As I was paying for the food, she said, "You are a very beautiful lady," and I smiled. I told her I took myself out for the first time today, and I enjoyed it. I just have to do it for myself. She laughed, and I said thank you very much. As I was driving home, I kept thinking about what the woman at the restaurant said, and I asked myself, "So, I am a beautiful woman?" I thanked God almighty, and then I went again to the shop and bought something for myself and drove home.

When I got home, I did not do anything; I sat down in the sitting room, crossed my legs with a small stool, and fell asleep. I didn't notice when my son came back. I only heard when he said, "Mama?"

I said, "Yes?"

He said, "You are not looking bad."

I said, "Thank you."

I told him I was not cooking today and that he should go to the pizza shop opposite the house and buy pizza for himself.

He did, and when he was eating, he said, "It's good at times to eat out, not cooking all the time."

I told him, "Yes, it's good." And though it's also expensive, we do it more often henceforth or look for a food shop that is not too expensive, buy the food and bring it home to eat, that we both deserve it.

Writer's intent

The story is to understand that most women in Africa single-handedly struggle throughout their lives to care for their family's needs, especially their children. The majority of black African women do not have help from their husbands, children's fathers, family or friends. They live a single-parent life even when married most often.

Most of these women are abandoned when they get pregnant. Even when the men take responsibility at first, they will still ask them to go live with their parents during pregnancy because they will say the symptoms irritate them. They will rather more frequently be with a new girlfriend outside their home, especially when they have little money to spend. While some of the men would rather abandon the women to be alone.

Most times, the woman's parents will not really understand the abandoning tricks of the African men because they are even happy that they are taking care of their daughter in their own home because she is expecting a baby.

If the woman lives in the village, a typical African village, she has to be very strong even with the pregnancy; she will have to work very hard, go to the farm, and walk a very long distance before getting there. If she has an older baby, she will have to wrap the older baby on her back with her protruded stomach to the farm. When she gets to the farm, she is meant to do all the farm work by herself and then carry the farm proceeds on her head back home. She gets home without resting and goes and prepares meals for her children and household.

So the life of an African woman is filled with hard labour. Most times, she is happy that she even has a man to call her husband and that the man is even magnanimous enough to give her farmland to fend for herself. But in the civilised world, it's regarded as a punishment that might cause complications in pregnancy for her.

When I look at the situation of my mother as an African woman and a single mother for most of her life, I am not pleased at all. Right from when she lived with her first husband, she had to struggle alone for the children because the husband had other wives, so every woman for herself.

It was more difficult for my mother because she didn't go to school and she was living in the city. If she had been in the village, it would have been easier because the struggle in an African village is cheaper than in the city. It was still a little easier for her because her mother was in the village, so she used to shuffle between the city and the village.

For my late sister Martha, the death of her husband brought about her single parenthood. The family of the man abandoned her and her son. She was left alone to cater for herself and her son till she died.

The African men living in Europe have a different attitude toward treating women better than the ones living in Africa, because they are afraid of the police. They know that African women in Europe will easily get help from the government for social welfare, and also, the majority of the men have jobs that they do to take care of their responsibility, likewise the women. They both know that it is good to respect each other and take care of their responsibility because they both know their fundamental human rights. But there are still some African men in Europe who still behave like African men living in Africa, like Raymond and Felix. They leave all responsibilities of the home and children for the woman to shoulder alone, thereby making the women single mothers, whether they are with a man or not. So the struggle continues for the black African woman.

The author

Philomena Schley was born in the ancient city of Benin, Edo State of Nigeria. On 12th Of October 1967. She is the eldest daughter of the family. Growing up was full of challenges, but her zeal for success made it interesting. She attended Benin Technical College, obtaining her O level certificate. Coming from a humble background and being raised by a single mother, she built herself with virtue and determination to turn things around for the good of all. She relocated to Germany in 1991 where she currently resides, working as a qualified nurse. She is blessed with three wonderful children.